I Wish Death Would Take A Vacation
The Story Continues
(A Mini Memoir)
Part Two

I Wish Death Would Take A Vacation
The Story Continues
(A Mini Memoir)
Part Two

Joy M. Mills

The Eyes of the Heart

Therefore consider carefully how you listen. Whoever has will be given more; whoever does not have, even what they think they have will be taken from them.

~ Luke 8:18 ~

Copyright © 2019 by Joy M. Mills

Library of Congress Number: 2019912064
ISBN-13: 978-0-9854367-2-8
ISBN-10: 0-9854367-2-7

All rights reserved.

The names of some individuals have been changed. Such names are indicated by an asterisk (*) the first time each appears in the narrative.

No part of this book may be reproduced or transmitted in any form or by any means, electronic or mechanical, including photocopying, recording, or by any information storage and retrieval system, without permission in writing to Joy Mills and Associates, LLC.

This book was printed in the United States of America.

Published by Lightsource Publications

This book is not intended to provide and does not constitute medical, legal or other professional advice. This book was written to support, not replace medical or psychiatric treatment. Please seek professional care if you feel you have a condition.

THICK AND THIN

I could skip a heartbeat
I would survive
I could be in a car crash
And still be alive
The clouds could fall
Out of the sky
The Ocean could disappear
And all turn dry

These things in life
Are all uncertain
There are far worse things
Just thought you should know

Life would not be the
Same without you
You are there
And so am I
To help each other through
Through the good times and bad
Happy or sad
I don't have to be right there
And neither do you

We could be apart for years on end
I really wouldn't want to
You and I would remain

Life goes on
People change
Through it all our friendship
Remains

Such as life how things
Come to be

Just thought you should know
How much you mean to me

Joy M. Mills
Copyright (c) 2017

Dedication

For my girlfriends, my tribe. You know who you are.

You have taught me to let someone love me, just the way I am, as flawed and unattractive as I feel at times and as unaccomplished as I thought I was. I no longer believe I must hide all of the parts of me that have been broken out of fear that someone else is incapable of loving what is less than perfect. Through the cracks the light comes in.

There is beautiful tension between dreams and happiness. As a full-on dreamer, I have quite a list of what I hope to accomplish with my writing. How do I deal with this in spite of life's uncertainty? I will define my sense of accomplishment not by a list of finished products or awards but by the way I spent the day, the day before and the days before that.

I am going to use the space to live the good stuff twice and learn from all of the rest to let it go and know I am enough. This is what we do for each other.

~J.M.

Contents

Dedication...	9
Introduction...	13
Acknowledgements..................................	15
Preface...	17
Chapter One: Door Number One.....................	21
Chapter Two: Me, Myself and I'm Not Sure..........	29
Chapter Three: Knock, Knock – Who is There......	35
Chapter Four: Full Circle...............................	41
Chapter Five: The Paradox............................	47
Chapter Six: Flights of Thought......................	53
Chapter Seven: Life....................................	63
Chapter Eight: You Owe Me a House...............	69
Chapter Nine: This is Not a Dress Rehearsal........	75
Chapter Ten: Upended................................	83

Chapter Eleven: A Godwink........................... 89

Chapter Twelve: Save a Seat at the Table............ 95

Chapter Thirteen: The Whole Universe is Yours... 101

Epilogue... 107

Afterword... 109

Bibliography... 111

Other Works by Joy M. Mills
(Including Bibliographic References)................... 113

Resources.. 117

What People Are Saying............................. 119

About the Author................................... 127

Introduction

The story continues.

Childhood gifted me with a number of unhealthy survival mechanisms which still follow me around today: a deep fear of conflict because for me conflict meant someone would leave. Constant apologies and guilt I am not responsible for and a voice in the back of my mind telling me no matter what I do, who I am, who I become, it will never be enough. It is one thing to forgive and move on from a wound we received in the past and another animal entirely when we get hurt again and again in the same place by the same people; a scab not quite healed over before it is ripped off.

What I am feeling is anger, unfairness, and aversion. Repressed feelings mean they will come up again at some point, most likely when another situation triggers a similar response. Negative emotions sap our energy, and that can spread like wildfire. I liken it to a single match burning down an entire forest. I do not want anybody to steal my ability to love and care.

Confronting someone who has hurt you can be a daunting and challenging task. Saying to another person, man or woman, what you said hurt my feelings, please do not do that again, is appropriate.

Here is what I know. The less you feed the bully, the less often, he or she will take your lunch. As always, being an example is our best teacher.

I am sorry is a statement admitting you are wrong and not letting your ego stand in the way. At times, it means nothing to say I am sorry, but it is a stepping stone to a future change.

I will not do it again is a promise. A promise is a debt so be careful when using your words. *How can I make it up to you* is a responsibility. Changing is difficult, not changing is fatal. I had to learn this the hard way. I do not always understand other people's actions, but actions speak louder than words.

Here is what I was forced to relearn: if I felt I treated others with respect, I would deserve the same. When times are tough, no pain comes without a purpose. Move on from what hurt you but never forget what it taught you. Everything is going to come together.

Acknowledgements

In this fractured time of home and hearth and heart, when the divide seems impossible to cross and the bridge you cannot see, you hold steadfast to all you have. Trust the process, look up and pray. Lean into your pain for a second or two. The truth is, all is not lost nor gone away. You'll need your strength and courage now. In time, the pain will ease. Look for others to show their love, and they will remind you of exactly who you are....

I would like to thank my husband, Larry, with yet another book, another project. You stand by, supportive, omnipresent, making me believe anything is possible. You have shown more courage than any thousand people, and you teach me every day of our walk together -- you have heart and soul and captured mine long ago.

My friends, you reach out and roll up your sleeves with whatever we are doing. I am so grateful all of you are a part of my life. You bring laughter, playfulness, and such a constant source of love for me – Alexa, Pam, Kara, Stefanie, Jenny, Lisa and Steve. I love you all (you know who you are).

And, to all the people who made this book possible, I appreciate your help, your input and hard work, late nights and long days. What special people you are! I thank God for all of you every day.

16 I Wish Death Would Take A Vacation – The Story Continues

I am a paradox of conflicting emotions after the loss of my mother, which is confusing. If I did not know it was normal to experience grief years after a loss, I think I would be feeling pretty crazy about now. It just rolls in like a slow-motion tsunami and carries you off down the shore. You might find yourself removed from the extreme intensity of grief as time goes by. The distance is a loss that needs to be grieved, but on the other side of the paradox is the reality that so many roads still lead back to her.

The story continues.

Preface

Faith and fear void each other out. It would have to be one or the other. It is the life you were given, not the life you expected.

Chances are at some point in time you have been taken advantage of by someone you trusted. You feel powerless to do anything about it. In the end, we cannot control other's behaviors.

The world does not owe you a thing. Your parents did not/do not owe you anything beyond raising you, and some do not do a good job at that. Your bosses do not owe you anything. You want something, you work hard and earn it. Do not expect anyone to do anything for you. If they do, that is a privilege, not an entitlement. Remember that. If you want respect, you have to give it.

Notice what happens when you disagree with a person and have said no. Their feelings can range from irritation, self-pity to full-blown rage. Do they pout or throw an adult size tantrum? While it is important to stand your ground on things that matter to you, if they react childishly, learn how to manage this carefully. Learn not so much how to disagree but fail to agree. You spend lots of precious energy trying to grab onto the edge of an ideal that does not exist.

There is a fine line between acknowledging their underlying need without buying into, "I am going to help you because you think I should." Unless you need a pillow fluffed, I would suggest leaving these kinds of people at the next stop. Real friends challenge and debate with real transparency. I found it takes both clear boundaries and a mindful shift and perspective to protect myself from others' emotions.

Relationships are an accumulation of life's continuous serendipity, but friendships are intentional.

I woke up one morning different; done trying to figure out who was with me, against me or just walking down the middle because they did not have the guts to pick a side. I was done with anything that did not give me peace.

I realized opinions were a dime a dozen, validation was for parking, and loyalty was not a word but a lifestyle. It was this day that my life changed. Not because of a person or a job but because I realized life was way too short to leave my keys in someone else's pocket.

Chapter One
Door Number One

> But he said to me, "My grace is sufficient for you, for my power is made perfect in weakness." Therefore I will boast all the more gladly of my weaknesses, so that the power of Christ may rest upon me. For the sake of Christ, then, I am content with weaknesses, insults, hardships, persecutions, and calamities. For when I am weak, then I am strong.
>
> ~ 2 Corinthians 12:9-10 ~

Door Number One

Everyone on the planet and I mean everyone has fears, and it is not something to be ashamed of; perfect people do not exist in the world. Standing at a crossroad, think of the worst possible outcome or worst-case scenario. You would still be able to find a way out and a direction to take unless your anchor, your savior, the person you leaned into most was just buried. My brother Joey was not coming back.

I was fourteen years old, grief-stricken, and in a fog. I found myself looking for something or someone. A fatherless girl thinks all is possible and nothing is safe. When my brother Joey died, I did not know what to do, but I had a boyfriend. It was a perfect storm for what would be my first marriage. That is what I believed.

I was running from yet another heartbreak, headlong into a very unclear future. Life is capricious. It breeds interruptions and imperfections regularly. You can rarely count on things going according to plan. The problem was I had no plan. Joey's death was consuming me, and nobody was noticing. They were too busy dealing with their brand of grief. My fear of abandonment was at an all-time high. If someone did not keep their word, even with the smallest of things, I found the depression, grief, and anxiety were causing me to throw up. The world was getting larger, and I wanted to disappear.

Enter door number one. I have always thought of relationships as a series of doors. If I did not like what was behind one, I would close it and open the next door.

I wanted to believe that my first ex-husband, Waldo, would be like my brother Joey as far as being my protector. In my fifteenth year of life, I found myself pregnant, ostracized by my church and everything that was already spinning out of control began to unravel faster. My church had taught staunch discipline, respect for the father, and women were to be seen and not heard.

The elders held an emergency meeting once my pregnancy was revealed, and the gauntlet fell. Other girls who were my friends were not allowed to talk with me as if the pregnancy was contagious. I was not allowed to attend any youth groups or activities, and God forbid if I made eye contact with anyone. I was suddenly a pariah and bought into the white picket fence idea in a hurry if it would give me a reprieve from Plymouth Brethren Jail and the Elders. I did not feel I had any other choices.

If God were ever to forgive me, I was going to have to follow their rules, which began with getting to know my boyfriend's mother to see if I was a satisfactory candidate to marry him, pregnant or not. By late summer, she decided I was approved to marry her son, and the wedding was on. However, we were not allowed to marry at the chapel but quietly at home. Then we were welcomed back into the chapel as a full-fledged married couple. Later that year, the women of the chapel planned a baby shower with cake and everything.

The honeymoon was at a hotel around the corner from his parent's home. Waldo* worked as a cook at this hotel. Back then, I thought I was happy, and the world was my oyster.

We remained in the basement of Waldo's parents' home until well after the birth of our son, and we both completed our high school educations. Waldo got a better job, and we moved into an apartment. The storm began brewing with the pressures of paying rent, having a young child, and the strain of the game of Where's Waldo, which included late nights of him disappearing. I learned later he met "new friends."

We found another apartment, even more luxurious than the first, and we stopped going to the chapel. Waldo did not see the point because someone from the chapel taught me to drive. He did not want me to have that kind of freedom, but guess what, I was getting older, had a young son, and I wanted a driver's license like everyone else. It was an act of defiance.

I was beginning to wonder why it was that women had to be subservient and what it was about me that Waldo felt it necessary to crush. After four years of marriage, we bought a house, Waldo received a better job, and I got part-time work. I no longer wanted to answer for a bottle of fingernail polish. As I look back on it now, I did not realize at the time I was beginning to outgrow the rules, the marriage, and the man.

At one point, I briefly moved out. Our fights were getting old, the lies were getting bigger, and patience was getting thinner. Waldo cut up my purse without provocation. I wanted to leave, so I put my child in his car seat, I got in the driver's seat, and Waldo poured gasoline or motor oil on both myself and my child and threatened to light us on fire.

During one of the times I had moved out from the marital home, the group at work encouraged me to come out with them. They were always having a celebration of some kind. Although I was not quite twenty-one, I felt by this time as if I was forty-five. I had partaken in the margaritas and shots for the first time in my life.

I needed a friend, and there was a new guy, a nice guy who showed me attention. It was a time of fear, desperation and love, the great motivators, and I needed someone, anyone to listen. I did not realize until decades later, that nice guy owned the company. God rest his soul. After one of our company get togethers, the nice guy offered up his couch because I was not in any shape to drive. My only experience of having sex outside of my marriage happened that night. Did I say liquor and love do not mix? Stay tuned.

Waldo showed up to the parking lot of my work within a week of my night out. He wanted to work our marriage out; I had a four-year-old asking about his daddy, Waldo was threatening to take my son and reminded me I was not twenty-one yet. As a matter of fact, I was twenty and some change. Plus, I was raised to believe you do not walk away, so I went back. When I look back on it now, I was so young and had been sheltered for a very long time.

Within two months of Waldo visiting the parking lot at work, I discovered I was pregnant. He made me quit my job. I was going to stay at home and be the Godly woman I was designed to be. It was a conundrum because I wanted my child but did not want the marriage. I was stuck somewhere in God's little acre, west of the rock and east of the hard place.

I knew I would have to wait until the birth of my second baby to escape. I believed I would rather live in a pup tent with my children than look at him one more day. I did not know how but knew I would be able to escape a marriage that should have never happened in the first place.

It took me a full year after having my second son to move out and file for divorce. It was not going to work. Strength is what we gain from the madness we survive.

Here is what I know now:

Life is a toilet, but technically we are the ones who fill it, and thus, we are full of it as well. The toilet is not a place of residence. You get to leave the toilet when you are finished, unlike real life when you do not know when it will be over.

Breaking the habit of yourself requires a heavy dose of appreciation. You show up every day at a job you hate. Your marriage makes you feel miserable. You hate where you live. How the heck did I get here? How the heck do I get out?

Everything shows up for us based on what we believe to be true, what we believe we deserve. There is nothing more preventative from moving ahead than living in the past and continuing negative stories we tell ourselves. Misfortune can be an incredible opportunity to notice we are stuck in the state of mind that will never lead to fulfilled desires. Adversity could be a wake-up call telling us we are out of harmony with the life we want.

I doubt that any of us have become masters of our Universe. Adversity and misfortune will probably end up in the mix of our daily life. We need to learn how to gain the maximum benefit from it. Maybe we feel like a shadow version of the person we know we are. If any of this sounds familiar to you, now is an excellent time to contemplate on what it is you want. Reassess your goals and remind yourself you are in the driver's seat of your life.

Stop trying to figure it out all on your own. The truth is sometimes we do not see what we are doing wrong, and we need someone else to point it out. It is usually embarrassingly obvious when we look at it, but we would have never noticed it if not for an expert or a friend offering us another perspective. You are not alone in your struggles. The same handful of issues repeat themselves in so many lives.

Put your insights into practice. You have to get clear on your purpose and vision. Thankfully, I woke up to who I really am. Beyond my body, thoughts, emotions, titles and roles, I discovered I was a soul in a body, not a body with a soul. I did not want to be his wife for one more minute.

Chapter Two
Me, Myself and I'm Not Sure

Narcissists are control freaks. They want to control everything in your life. What you look like, whom you talk to and where you go. They will always try and change you to what they want you to be. They shift the blame. Everything they did was because someone else made them do it and will take no responsibility for their actions.

Narcissists avoid problems until they get out of hand. You or someone else was the reason for it.

Me, Myself and I'm Not Sure

Liquor and love do not mix. Add a narcissist to the mix, shake vigorously and welcome to hell.

My first marriage began as a cloistered world and became a slow train to hell with one pit-stop that stands out which I will address later in this book.

Shortly after my first divorce, I met a man who was funny, intriguing and loved to expose me to everything different to the way I lived prior. He wanted to fix things for me. He wore a uniform, so I thought he was stable, secure and a gift from the Universe. He was older than me.

People are drawn to the light, that force within us all. The energy which flows through us. Love is the aspect of ourselves that we seek. It lies within all of us, and if we are unable to find it, we look to others.

Early on I did not know we were going to dance the narcissist tango. Then, we got married. What a mistake.

Within the first month of marriage, I was driving a vehicle that was struck by an intoxicated driver. That accident left me with two fractured vertebrae at my brain stem. Those had to be fused together, and the recovery process took a full year. A nurturer he was not. One of the most difficult things to understand is how someone who professes to love you, can abuse you. It starts verbally and gradually gets violent.

I felt so devalued. I had two small children to take care of while mending my broken body. They were living with their father. That is how bad it had become in our home. I could not even feed them without assistance. Let us say his emotional empathy tank ran low, let alone actually helping me. I hit an all-time low and was becoming depressed. I wanted a divorce five minutes after our wedding. The grand epiphany was this marriage and the first were failures to launch. He was commenting on things like my dress being too short, and then the accident happened.

One of the reasons people abuse others they have professed to love is they lack empathy. Add serious alcoholism to the mix and it spells disaster.

Door Number Two,* second ex-husband, lacked the capacity for empathy. He was more willing and able to emotionally and physically hurt someone, and he did.

I got a house. My kids came back to live with me. I was healthy again; graduated from college and felt I could set the world on fire. Somehow, all of the earlier turmoil was just because of the accident, or so I told myself.

What had been fun and exciting had gradually degenerated to dangerous. My husband walked in and announced he quit his job, he was too stressed and expected me to take care of him. He was now spending his days drinking. I was beyond tears. I had experienced everything from sadness, terror, humiliation, and degradation. It was a downhill slide, and there was nothing left. It was time to go.

I realized my husband's feelings for me were not born of love. They had become an obsession. Unconditional love is not possessive. He, like my first husband, had tried to own me, sap my energies, strip me of my identity and make me into what he wanted me to be.

I knew exactly when it was finished. Something inside me clicked off as if it were a lightbulb and someone reached up and pulled the silver chain; the marriage was left in utter darkness. I knew if I stayed I would become as sick or sicker than he was. You are only as sick as your deepest secret. I found the courage and filed for divorce.

Here is what I know now:

The truth is, you knew exactly what you had. You just did not think that you were going to lose it.

Everyone has a story. Do not get lost in the white noise. We get our hearts hurt. We get insulted. We allow the hurt to linger too long. We take people for granted.

When someone abandons or rejects you, it is more about them than yourself. Your heart will get broken. You will come up empty and disappointed. Life can hurt, and people will fail you. Having a meltdown or breakdown is okay as long as you decide not to unpack and live there.

Here is the thing: a self-fulfilling prophecy is when we focus on the negatives and draw them to us like moths to a flame. The same thing holds true for positives. What is required of you is you have to do the work by having a tremendous will and forgiveness to overcome childhood abandonment or any other hideous thing that may have happened to you. It is not easy.

Have hope and the ability to reach higher and go further when the deck seems stacked against you. We all are capable of change, love, and forgiveness.

Logically, the process and progress of letting go is not the end of the world; it is a beginning of a new life. There are things we never wanted to let go of or people we never wanted to leave behind.

Letting go in and of itself seems very broad. It can apply to everything from taking a deep breath, or relinquishing the desire to "control" a situation.

Life and God have grander plans for you that do not involve crying all night or believing you are broken. We relive it over and over, letting the offenders live rent-free in our heads.

Chapter Three
Knock, Knock – Who is There

There is a myth that everybody is sold sometime in his or her life. It goes like this: you have a bucket of anger, and when it gets full, you need to pour it out - and that will be cathartic. Just let it go.

The problem is you do not have a bucket of anger in your life. These days, it seems we have created a factory of rage. A factory can keep producing, producing and producing. That aggression only creates more fury. Angry outbursts lead to more anger more often than not until it begins a habitual pattern.

Knock, Knock – Who is There

I had filed for divorce, and it was not yet final. The thing about abusers, they keep coming. Nothing would ever be enough. I thought the love I gave him was enough. Later I would compare our marriage to drowning victims. He had stepped on me, the rescuer, hoping for more, the more that would never be enough, and when he stepped on me, he had drowned us both.

The problem was that my oldest son, although only fourteen or so at the time, was going under with us. My soon to be ex in typical narcissistic style, figured he could fix everything.

My oldest son had several friends spending the night, and my youngest son was spending the night away at a friend's home. I worked late that night and was bone tired. I ordered pizza for the boys and retired to my bedroom. Then I heard it. The basement door was crashing open. In my half sleep state, I wondered if the wind had blown the door open.

Imagine my shock when I opened my bedroom door and stood face-to-face with this man who was in a drug-induced jealous rage. He asked, "Who were you talking to at work tonight?" This, just before he began to pound on me. I did not hear much as he was busy rearranging my face, blow by blow. He threw me onto the bed and grabbed one of the posts, breaking the frame. All of this as I tried to explain, "I was only working."

My oldest son was standing behind the maniac. I heard a guttural, angry, fierce scream, coming from my son, like I have never heard before, "Get off of my mother!" I looked to see him standing with four of his friends, all holding bats and meaning business. The soon to be ex told them, "This does not involve you!" But the boys did not back down. He left, but not before announcing he would be back. He did go, using the front door and one of the boys called the police.

I was taken to the hospital with a ruptured eardrum, along with other various injuries. They found him around the corner threatening to kill me on a payphone with a female officer standing directly behind him, hearing every word. He was then arrested.[1]

I was numb, exhausted and trying to process what happened when I did make my way home after being treated. I apologized to my son for having to see that ugly display. All I could think was that I was dragging my sons through this nightmare.

I sent my sons again to stay with their father. I did not want them to see anything like that again. I changed the locks and was trying to find a way to tell my family what happened. We went to court, and the judge granted not only the divorce but a full order of protection. He was criminally charged and pleaded no contest. I never saw the man, the myth or the legend again. There must be angels in heaven.

Walking away from the courthouse that day, I came to realize that enough was enough, that I had done my best, I was drawing a line in the sand. Continually trying to hold him up was emotionally exhausting, and I kicked him to the curb.

---

[1] No two sets of circumstances are the same. Domestic violence is a national crisis. The National Domestic Violence Hotline is 1-800-799-7233.

Here is what I know now:

With eyes full of clarity, you are capable of changing the relationships in your life by adjusting your point of view.

When you are not a priority, it stings. Unfortunately, timing is a harsh mistress. Do not assume people will respond to things as you will. You will set yourself up and hurt yourself the most. Stop living in a fantasy land of hope and assumptions. That reality will leave you feeling empty. If you are aware of the truth, people cannot manipulate situations.

People like this do not mind disappointing you. They do not put much effort into meeting your needs. The sun goes around the earth at the same rate of speed for everyone. We are all busy, but good relationships require quality time. You want the outcome to exceed expectations and have a positive impact. When it does not, it is sad.

Get out of the fantasy world by not hooking into the thoughts of what could be. The hard part is to let it go. Throw expectations and assumptions out the door. Focus on those who genuinely love you. If you remind yourself of those who are there for you, they continue to be there because they care about you.

Focus on people who make you feel loved, connected and worthy.

WHAT YOU ALLOW WILL CONTINUE

"No offense" means I am
about to insult you
but do not get mad.
A person's insecurity
inflicted on you is sad.

If we learn
our lessons and share
them well, there would be no
more insults or things to tell.

"No offense" means
I am about to insult you but
you did not do anything wrong.
You just started to change
and grow and some
cannot come along.

Their journey is different.
The crossroads are there.
Others will be happy
and others will not care.

Some will be miserable,
dishonorable and take until
you are through.

"No offense" if it is not true.
I know my heart.
What about you.

Joy M. Mills
Copyright © 2018

Chapter Four
Full Circle

Many offenses are personal. Let us be clear; do not confuse forgiveness with reconciliation. Reconciliation is a beautiful, magical, redeeming experience if it happens. Forgiveness is for you and your heart without the other person's participation. It is not an eraser that will wipe away the pain that has happened to you.

Full Circle

Today I am going to forgive myself.

The time between the physical abuse incident and the divorce were some of the most difficult, challenging days and weeks. As a mother, I was emotionally spent, spiritually broken, and I knew none of this would be any good for my children.

My firstborn son, my child, one of the great loves of my life, bore witness to something he should have never seen. My youngest son, the other great love of my life, needed to be kept safe. These were the things that kept me awake at night. I knew I not only had to inform their father about went on, a challenge all by itself, but decisions were going to have to be made for their well-being and safety.

Make no mistake - I knew I was going to send them back to live with their father to keep them safe from the insanity that became my life. There was no other choice. I did not turn them over to strangers or Social Services, but their father. Albeit he was a jerk, but it was a conclusion we came to for the best interests of our children.

At this juncture, my life was becoming unhinged. I was doing well to put one foot in front of the other and to form a sentence or two. I knew I was not going to be able to turn this around in a day, week or month.

Waldo pulled up to the house with a truck, and I knew it would be full by mid-afternoon with all of my boys' worldly possessions. It broke my heart, but it was the right decision considering I did not know where their next meal would be coming from or how long I would be able to keep my house, given the current state of affairs.

I had a full-circle moment. I sold all of my possessions trying to do damage control and was forced to move in with relatives; this did not last long. What I knew was I could go to my mother and stepfather but, oh, I did not want to. The last time I had anything to do with my parents in this manner, I was divorced, working full-time, and going to school, and they helped me watch my kids, my youngest in particular. Not for free, of course. I had to pay them. To the rest of the world, it looked like he lived there, and during the week, he did.

When I moved back in, which was more than okay with my mother and stepfather, for a price, the other job had ended so I got a job doing office and title work at a car lot. What I knew when I moved in, I was going to work as hard and quickly as possible to get myself out of there.

I was reading for people here and there. It was more of a hobby. It certainly was not my career, after all, I had a degree. As if that made me important.

My stepfather did me a favor at this time. He started talking about my gift and continued to talk about my gift. People were still coming and going for readings in an office I set up in the basement. What my stepfather said and it resonated with me, "You are good at this. People are happy; they keep coming and are referring people to you. I don't know why you don't do this full-time. Yours is a gift from God. You aren't a gypsy or anything." My response was, "I don't know about all of that. I have a job, responsibilities, and don't want to live here until the end of time."

At the end of a full year, even after paying rent and my kids' expenses, I was able to save enough money to move into an apartment in St. Charles. What did help, the car lot provided me a loaner car to drive, a significant bonus.

Here is what I know now:

Divorce sucks. If I were writing a letter and I am supposed to be loving me first, should not the letter be addressed as "It is I?" I would address the letter as, "Joy, wake up. How have you been?"

I have been on quite a journey. I hugged my knees, cried for hours until the tears dried, and then I started to cry again. I sat there on the floor in a daze at the stormy situation around me. The fear was palpable, and the pain was real. It was heart-wrenching pain.

Life is never a straight line. Calamities and hardships are your greatest blessings. You know, the lessons in disguise. The difficulties, the unexpected, forces us into a new and better version of ourselves. You are made to survive the hardest days of your life. I choose to live life on purpose. Here is to today and the years that await me and no matter what life serves up, may I be grateful through it all.

Some years back, I had a grand epiphany. What I have learned is you have to stop giving so much of yourself to people who cannot even identify who they are. If these people do not sacrifice for you, then they should gain nothing from you. Things of value require sacrifice. It is a work in progress.

If people are too hurt, too busy or just too damned stupid to see you are the blessing they have been asking for, then fall back. I know my worth. I deserve happiness, I deserve respect, and I deserve love. I have everything I need.

Deep down I am still haunted by past experiences. I know there is still unfinished business. I hope there is a resolution one day. I am grateful for the life I have now. It is my life, and I would not change a thing. If you want to hear God laugh, tell Him your plans for the day.

Everyone has a story, and no two stories are the same. Remember, there are over seven billion people in this world, and none of them are like you. Your entire life journey is a series of footprints that have brought you to this very moment in time. Life is a tapestry of people weaving in and out of your life for a reason, a season or a lifetime. Every one of them has something to offer and share with you.

Chapter Five
The Paradox

Moms fall into two distinctive categories: those whose mothers are alive and well, and those whose mothers are neither. Mine, however, was alive but unwell; she was here and physically present but absent in every way that counted.

I have learned the hard way no one throws a wake or sits Shiva for an ambiguous loss. As a mother myself, I have to take a step back, take a deep breath and extend myself some grace.

The Paradox

In time, however, you will learn to forgive your mother, albeit imperfectly, for what she could not give you. More importantly, forgive yourself for what you were not given.

My mother's death forced me to realize I was still angry over the lot I had been given early in my life. It is reflective. I had a mother who lacked the capacity to love me unconditionally and an absent father.

As a child, my mother and the adults around me set me up for a life of low self-esteem, the insidious belief I would never be good enough and believing I did not deserve to be loved. I carried terrible shame of coming from people who did not give me the support and the tools I needed as a child and still struggle with as an adult.

When I have slipped back into anger, it is because I do not feel strong enough to leave the pain behind and accept the blessings in my life. Everything was complex: the humiliation of emotional and physical abuse and the stigma of being damaged coming from a place of adults who did not protect me. I still deal with the occasional nightmares.

Back then, it made me question the ability to be a good mother because of how I grew up; the awful fear of not being strong enough to break the cycle. If you have not experienced this, you cannot understand my emotional turmoil. You may nod your head and offer a word of support and understanding, but secretly, I still feel you are judging me.

My question is and always has been: how could a mother shun her children? What I have realized now, though, is when I was a young mother, the damage I must have unknowingly inflicted on my sons. I have learned that mothers do not take love away as fast as they give it. They do not threaten to abandon their children. They do not take their anger out on their children. They can handle important life events without punishing their children for their happiness. They actually revel in their children's achievements instead of lashing out.

Was I perfect? No, no mother can tell you that with a straight face. It took me years to not cave into the pain I carried around even with all of the good around me. I was young, but as I write this now, I have zero doubt I was a horrible mother. They will be stronger in their relationships, and their lives will be better than mine. This has always been my prayer for them. Amongst the anger and the terrible pain, there is immense gratitude.

Door Number Three, my precious Larry, opened up my whole world, the real deal, was sent to help me heal, to show me what love really should be: not conditional, not manipulative, not controlling. He may not always like me, but he still loves me and is there for me.

Learning to show my children the love and affection I never received was like winning the lottery. I am not my mother! The past will always haunt you. Is there such a thing as starting over? A clean slate many seek to attain, but many fail to achieve.

Every decision we make in our lives has an impact on our future, regardless of how large or small it is. It is unavoidable and problematic because at one moment something may seem like a good idea, but somewhere down the road it can come back to bite you in the ass.

Some decisions you choose to make have dire consequences that will follow you for the rest of your life. No matter how hard I have tried, my past always seems to be nipping at my heels. Certain experiences will trigger emotional responses that will bring you back to your past, and you have no choice but to relive those memories. Things do mold you and make you who you are. At the same time, some decisions can haunt you for the worse. Bad relationships can be traumatizing, and the effects they have on your psyche can and most often do follow you into future relationships.

We all take our licks. We feel like we ought to be able to write our own scripts to our lives. At times, we feel disappointed in God when life rewrites the plot. The key is acceptance and gratitude. We need to practice wanting what we have, not what we wish we had.

Here is what I know now:

Like every human being on this planet, myself included, the hard days are necessary to live through and learn from, and the hardest days make us who we are inside and out. You cannot find peace by avoiding life. Life spins with unexpected changes. Take every change and experience as a challenge for growth. Either it will give you what you want or teach you what the next step is.

People may have heard your stories, and they believe they know you. They cannot feel what you are going through, much less understand where you have been. They are not living your life, so forget what they think and say about you.

Life and death are both essential parts of this messy journey, and to really live, we must show up for it all. Show up fully and receive with open arms the simple gifts of an ordinary day. Your mind slows down, your heart expands, and you remember today is enough.

The gift is now. The trick is to make the very best of it and value it for what it is worth. In other words, do not wish all of your time away waiting for better days ahead. Laugh and play because you can. That way, every moment is a new beginning.

Chapter Six
Flights of Thought

When your childhood memories are steeped in chaos and trauma, it does not mean no good things ever happen to you; it does mean you have a difficult time recalling them.

Instability meant family traditions went to the wayside, and day-to-day survival was all that mattered.

Flights of Thought

I had nothing to pass down, not a recipe, barely an heirloom, or some loving story. To manufacture a happy childhood from scratch for my children would have been hard work. At the time, there were just layers of hostility. I decided when they were born, they would always know how much I wanted them, they were loved, and college was non-negotiable, degrees were a must. I learned I was not a failure for having been victimized by the adults around me. The fact I was questioning myself along the way meant I had the makings of a good mother. It was trial and error.

My mother had flights of thought. I wondered for many years whether I would inherit that family curse. Until I read my mother's medical records, as many as I could get my hands on, I had not realized she was a product of years of the ever-evolving mental health field.

In hindsight, ignorance is bliss. I wondered what kind of life I wished on my poor innocent children. Perhaps, more fundamentally, was it selfish of me that I could be passing down a terrible legacy? Even if I had known, what could I do about it now?

I was a wreck making up holiday traditions. I would think about it but came up empty-handed.

One of the joys of being human is we do not have to be perfect to be one of the good ones. As a parent, the word "estrangement" was not in my vocabulary before it happened to me in 2015. And like many parents, I was ashamed and reluctant to talk about it. I have discovered 68% of those who are estranged to a family member believes there is a stigma attached to it. Once I started researching it, I realized I was not alone.

My older son and I had a typical mother and son relationship. I believed it to be close and loving. I could always count on him if the driveway had snow on it, if the computer had a malfunction in it or just for a laugh or hug.

My son was well educated, well-traveled, and had left to pursue his career out of the country where he met his present wife. After two years overseas, he was finally coming home. There was not one person who knew him or me that was not excited, so we planned a party.

Everyone gathered at my house while a close friend and I went to collect my son, his wife and her child from the airport. I had butterflies. The good news, the plane arrived early. My friend and I stood outside the security checkpoint, waited and waited and waited. Security and police were looking for them because their luggage had not been picked up. They called his name over the loudspeaker several times.

My friend and I decided to wait by their luggage as I called several different agencies to see if my son had perhaps missed the flight or one of his connections. His luggage made it, but maybe he didn't. The airline confirmed my son was on the plane. I looked up at the escalator, and there they were, finally. He looked so distraught and angry. The first thing he said and asked me in an angry tone was, "Why did you page me?" Holding back my tears, I said, "I didn't, they did," pointing to two police officers.

When his wife and I were first introduced over skype, I remember her face lighting up. I know it sounds cliché, but I remember thinking she was cute as a button, and she was. I was thrilled my son had someone to love and be loved back.

My son and his family lived in my house for seven months before moving into their own apartment, and his anger did not dissipate. Then, one day, I received a phone call from him that made no sense from the moment we started to the moment we hung up. The last thing he ever said to me four years ago, "I am going to abandon you, Mom, before you abandon me," and he did. I was reeling, but a clear rejection is better than a fake promise.

For me, motherhood has been and continues to be a rollercoaster of emotions, some good and some not so good. It has been a journey of loving, learning, and being humbled every single day.

Estrangement triggers so much shame, especially when the answer you are left with is - I am not sure. It feels like everyone is making judgments about you. Believing you must have done some awful thing. There were people close to me that had made statements that were supportive and kind because it was unbelievable based on the relationship my son and I had. My thought was I do not know, but I am not going to say anything bad about anybody.

How could someone you have loved their whole life act this way? I walked around in a daze. Every time the phone rang, my heart would jump, thinking it had to be him, and this cannot be happening. He is going to call. But when it was not him, it was a sense of relief. He had been so cold, and I could not bear the thought of hearing that angry tone in his voice again.

It was more painful than you could imagine. I had to learn to accept a new normal. It was clear my son had changed. It seemed he was done with us, and we could not fix it even if we wanted to. I wondered for a time if everyone else would leave me too? I was a basket case, and it has left a gaping hole and a broken heart that may never heal.

My son had so much anger. It was pitiful and bizarre. It was as if Invasion of the Body Snatchers had taken my son and ran off with him, this wonderful, loving and genuine person. The fear of abandonment is common for estranged parents. You devote your entire life to your child, and if they can leave, anyone else can. I remember many nights lying in the darkness, thinking of all the time and energy I wasted crying over a grown adult who wanted to be anywhere that his family was not. I could not help but think about how much time I had wasted. I had worn my husband out, my other child, and even some of my friends with sadness. They missed the old optimistic Joy, and so did I.

Sometimes people judge me. They say they would never give up on their child. I understand their feelings, but sometimes giving in to an adult child's decision is the only sensible choice. I wish my son the best. I genuinely hope he is happy and well, but I count too. What I want you to understand is if you can let go of all the whys and what-ifs and move on to what is next, you can live a fulfilling life.

I would say if he knocked on my door tomorrow, I would open it. I have been forced to love him from a distance, wherever he may be.

Strength is what we gain from the madness we survive.

Here is what I know now:

I hate every cliché about forgiveness. Forgiveness is a vast untraversable land for those of us that crave justice. The very thought of letting someone walk away scot free makes me sick.

I can see all of your faces the moment I say I am writing about how to forgive someone who never gave an apology. When people treat you like they do not care, believe them. Today I decided to forgive you not because you apologized or because you acknowledged the pain you caused me but because I deserve peace.

Many offenses are personal. Let us be clear: do not confuse forgiveness with reconciliation. Reconciliation is a beautiful, magical, redeeming experience if it happens. Forgiveness is for you and your heart without the other person's participation. It is not an eraser that will wipe away the pain that has happened to you.

The wrong way to apologize for me is when somebody will justify, minimize, excuse their behaviors or not say anything. The right way to apologize is to acknowledge, accept and express. I am not talking about a quick fix to years of pain. We all need to start looking simply to arrive at our best possible selves.

Forgiveness is reclaiming your power. The misery you will feel is heart-breaking. Your soul hurts, your body feels tortured, you do not sleep, and your mind is shattered. You lose your power when you feel abandoned.

You cannot control what other people do. We can only control how we react to them even if they never know. Either we choose to empower or disempower ourselves with our reactions.

Forgiving a person does not mean you have to trust them or forget what they did. You do not have to stay there in the replay of the pain. You can move on.

Forgiveness is the final step in a healing process. When we let go of our painful past, we make way for a bright and hopeful present and future. Forgiveness is the ultimate expression of love; the best gift we give ourselves.

A BROKEN PIECE

You would say I am
Overreacting
You didn't invite me
So I begin again
And I am finally free

The secret is
There will be no peace
In your lives
When you intentionally
Hurt others
That is not kind

You complained
About each other
Until I thought I would die
This I will not miss
Nor bother nor cry

I am better
Even when you use
Love and respect as
Words for me
They don't hold meaning
They are forever gone
But I will leave you
Alone and let it be

I am content with myself
I refuse to defend
I will stand as tall as I can
And have peace in the end

I will have to be content
With the way you are

I won't hear your moans or
Groans
I will move on and
Leave you behind

So I take heed from
This awful quest you have
Put me on
My heart may fall into
Pieces
My love will always be

I sit here and cry for
You
Not me

Joy M. Mills
Copyright (c) 2018

Chapter Seven
Life

Anxiety is a powerful thing. It is akin to an electric shock to the heart that shoots through your body with such vehement strength it propels you into the air. Being in constant fight or flight starts to feel like you just ran a marathon without training.

Life

At the end of 2014, my youngest son asked me to join him for dinner. I did not realize that my world was getting ready to spin off its axis. We finished dinner, and I thought it was nice having some alone time with my son. He stared at his hands and then quietly looked at me. He asked, "Mom, who is my father?" I said, "Unfortunately, you know who he is."

Did you grow up in a family where secrets were kept from you? Were these secrets truly hidden, or did everyone know or suspect something hidden? My son's next statement, "I have DNA, Waldo is not my father."

Flabbergasted does not begin to explain how I was feeling or what I was thinking at that moment. I said to my son, "That is a lie." I did not know or even believe it. I thought it was another chapter of a continuous attack from Waldo, who is known as a narcissistic monster where any woman was concerned, specifically me. He was not going to win any father of the year awards.

Earlier in this book, I spoke about a man I had encountered at work when I was separated from Waldo. I mentioned liquor and love do not mix. One of the most toxic problems confronting many families is the existence of secrets that prevent open communication. My son was going to continue to ask. My head was spinning. Was my son punking me? His eyes told me something different. I was grappling.

It is important to stress some secrets are better not to reveal if it were to cause unnecessary damage with no benefit. An extramarital affair, separated or not, was something I did not feel necessary to share with anyone ever. In particular, with my grown sons.

Let me be clear; my son did not go to get the DNA test to be malicious towards me. He wanted to prove to Waldo that he was his father so he would shut up. Waldo had been at my youngest son for awhile about how he is such a good guy. After all, he claimed he helped raise my youngest son knowing he wasn't his father.

When I finally could regain enough composure to speak, I recalled thinking back thirty-six years to the one and only man that it could have been. I gave my son the name. From there, it took my son eighteen months to finally reach out to that person's family. My son's wife had research to do first.

I came home, and after a couple of days of gut-wrenching crying, I grappled with the idea it could even be true. I was in shock. First, I spoke to my husband. He said, "It is in your past. How is our son doing?" I said, "Our son says he is okay." My husband gave me a hug and a kiss and said, "Waldo puts a whole new spin on evil. Who thinks of these things."

After a few days, I gathered all of my trusted friends, who are highly intelligent and educated and told them. We discussed this situation at length, and I asked them what they thought. I stood in my truth and tears. I was devastated for my son and me. Everyone rallied around me. If it were true, we would deal with it together. My only concern was how my son was going to weather this. When the DNA results came back showing Waldo was not his biological father, it all made sense to both my son and me. They are nothing alike.

One of my friends said to me, "You are not that little girl anymore. I am not going to let you punish yourself over something you did not know and can no longer control." But there was nothing pleasant about Waldo ever. My sentence would have been suspended by years had I known my youngest son was not biologically Waldo's. I would have never allowed Waldo to be anywhere near him.

Here is what I know now:

Let's be honest. If you are not currently enjoying your life and you are not waking up every morning with a sense of excitement, you need to do something about it. You deserve to live a good life.

We all have that one friend or family member (past or present) who is a constant drain on our energy. You want to keep that person in your life or may have to, but you could do without the huge amount of stress. While you cannot change who someone is, you can do a lot to remove the dysfunction from the situation. It is delicate. There are methods for staying sane for when the crazy train comes crashing into town.

What to do with the high maintenance people? They live in a world that revolves around them. They require a lot of time, money and effort. So, the only schedule that works for them is their own. They talk themselves up, they talk others down, and they will often forget or ignore the times you might need support.

It may be hard to know why someone may say or do something designed to hurt your feelings. If you do happen to be at the receiving end of this, do not let anyone else's behavior change who you are. How many times do you have to remind yourself not to take it personally? People will judge you, hurt you and put you down to try and break you. Most often, this will have nothing to do with you.

What I have learned is I can acknowledge their feelings, but I do not have to buy into them. Even if people like this are shown to be wrong, they will not apologize and feel they owe you nothing. They will justify their behavior as examples of their strength and other favorable attributes. They will become defensive.

Life is capricious. It breeds interruptions and imperfections regularly. You can rarely count on things going according to plan, but you can plan for potential problems and handle them well.

You should not brag, but you should not be afraid to stand for what is good about you. It does not mean you have to tell people these things directly. The number one way to stop others from taking advantage of you is by setting clear, enforceable boundaries. You might get brushed aside, but someone reminded me, "You are a diamond, dear. They can't break you."

Chapter Eight
You Owe Me a House

Some people will never like you because your spirit irritates their demons.

You Owe Me a House

My life was upended. I am just a little girl from Charlieville trying to manage my relationships; working harder not to allow them to manage me.

I think updating your narrative, seeing yourself as enough, not being so hard on yourself, not driving yourself crazy, not listening to the naysayers is so important. It took me sixty-plus years to learn this. The world does that to you. It brings me joy to share my story, the dark and the light of it.

Even today, I feel people close to me may be skeptical of whether or not a twenty-year-old would know who the father was of their child. In 2019, perhaps that is true but not in 1979. I had a mother who was born in 1928. We did not speak of such things. There were no sex or birth control talks, and your menstruation was off-limits. After all, my grandmother referred to a period as "The Curse – Eve ate the apple." Details of those things were shut down. I was criticized.

When you keep criticizing your kids, they do not stop loving you; they stop loving themselves.

I love to spend time with my family and friends. During one gathering, an individual brought up a situation from my past. It was my past, not hers. She used it as a segue, again, to ask a question and refused to believe my answer, which is the truth, and the more I think of it, none of her business. All the while, attempting to draw comparisons, except there were none. What I wanted to say is, "Work on yourself. Do not drag me into your misery." Damaged people love you like a crime scene before it ever gets cleaned up because they have already seen hell.

I am not going to waste time explaining myself to people who have proven that they are committed to misunderstanding me - asking the same questions disguised as other questions, expecting to get a different answer. I stand in my truth. I am not ashamed of my scars. They all have long since healed and continue to heal.

Each scar tells a story. I am not afraid to tell it, nor am I afraid to own it. Sadly, some people will not be happy until they have tried to push you into the ground metaphorically and stomp on you. No one should have that power, and if they do, take it back.

When a person keeps asking you the same question over and over, hoping for a different answer, maybe the reply should be, "I like that story better. Let's spin it that way."

I am going to pontificate. The pregnancy with my second son was not like my other pregnancies. There was monthly bleeding. The typical morning sickness did not come on until later, and to top it off, an older pompous doctor told me he would buy me a house if I were pregnant.

When I returned six weeks later with the same symptoms and what looked like breakthrough bleeding, they told me I was pregnant. I had to get a blood test and wait several days for it to come back. I told my doctor, his partner owed me a house. It still did not click in my twenty-year-old brain that anyone else other than my husband at the time could have been involved; after all, I was too busy trying to convince a doctor I was indeed pregnant.

I had several miscarriages prior to that. I think the doctors thought I just wanted to be pregnant or suffered from histrionics. Well, that pregnancy resulted in a son, who today is thirty-nine years old. This is the last time I will write about or speak of how my son came to be. What I will tell you is I love him very much.

My relationships are private, not secret. There is a tremendous difference. After all, my life has been a game of chess, not checkers.

Here is what I know now:

The soul is steadfast. It continues to thirst until the whole truth arrives. Left unsatisfied, the thirst of our souls results in a kind of spiritual death. We must be true to ourselves.

There are those rare individuals you would describe as "pathological truth-tellers." Those people forego socially convenient and appropriate fibs to speak the unvarnished upsetting truth.

Honesty should not feel like you are killing Bambi. Do not ask if you do not want to know. If I had one prayer right now, based on where the world is and how most of us live our lives, the prayer would be, "Remind me of what I have forgotten and inform me of Your will. I am ready and willing to know the truth."

We have all mastered the wrong lessons at some point in our lives. We have not asked for exactly what we want. We do not say what we mean. We avoid saying things so as not to upset other people.

What I am finding these days is many people entertain changes in their minds as a kind of fantasy or an ideal. In fact, in reality, it lies within your power.

Maybe this is what heals us: facing pain, looking it straight in the face but beyond all of that, finding there are blessings all mixed up in it. We lose our way only to find a deeper meaning.

Personal understanding lies far beneath the surface. Find the place of "Center," then remain there awhile.

You are responsible for you and only you. The truth is we have to be firm, fair and consistent. Everyone deserves second chances but not for the same mistake.

Truth is like surgery. It hurts but cures. A lie is like a painkiller. It gives instant relief but can have side effects forever.

Chapter Nine
This is Not a Dress Rehearsal

People will do whatever they want regardless of your feelings. Once you realize that, you will be free.

This is Not a Dress Rehearsal

It is a sign, it is time to grow, level up, to shift to something bigger. No matter how much it hurts, one day, you will look back and realize your struggles changed you for the better. Not all storms come to disrupt your life; some come to clear your path. I cannot tell you why I am not a statistic based on my upbringing, lack of guidance, and indifference of those around me.

I met a woman, and at the time, I did not realize she was going to open doors for me. The foundation for my career was already laid out, so I believed. Reading for people was something I did part-time to be of service, in the neighborhood of twenty years. I certainly did not want to do it full-time. Back then, it reminded me of being a glorified social worker. I came to realize God had a much bigger plan for me than I had for myself.

This woman said to me as she was giving me a reading, "I don't know why you are sitting in front of me. I should be sitting in front of you. You need to join us. There is room for everybody." Next, she asked me, "What do you think about doing Psychic Fairs or Expos?" My comment was, "Not much." Bear in mind; I was still paying back student loans from my life plan. My degree did not cover this - plot twist. I told this woman I would think about it half-heartedly.

I went home and had a conversation with my then-boyfriend, now husband. His comment was, "Why not, people are drawn to you. You seem to calm them. It is on a Saturday. You can do anything you want. I don't know much about it, but who am I to judge." Larry has always been my strongest supporter. Somehow, I received a pass and a table into an Expo. People came, and they kept coming.

My phone was ringing off the hook, one referral after the other. I have never advertised. I was forced to decide whether or not to do this part-time or full-time. There was no way I could work the equivalent of two full-time jobs, take care of the needs of my children, have a boyfriend, and keep up this kind of pace. My day would end at 11 p.m. and start at 6 a.m. with readings. Talk about no life. My choices were to do this work full-time, part-time or not at all.

The next thing I knew, I found myself on television and radio and speaking in front of large groups of people. My career was born, not the one I planned for but the one God intended for me.

For all of my life, I had been floating on a dingy in the middle of a hurricane. Somehow, I was dead center in the eye, found the shore and my way to safety.

Here is what I know now:

A clairvoyant does not have an incredible way of releasing you from the anchor of your sadness. However, with my age, wisdom and life experience, I do have the ability to listen carefully and empathize and sympathize. What I try not to do is draw comparisons. My personal life and journey have nothing to do with yours. If we intersect, it is because there is a message or a lesson in it. I come to a session honestly and open. It is not my job to draw you a beautiful picture or to scare you to death. Either one of those would be wrong.

A lot of people do not know what a clairvoyant is which is clear seeing, clear feeling and clear hearing. My role as a clairvoyant is to provide insight and to give information. We have free will and choice. I do not decide for anyone. Mine is a conversation with the person in front of me. I am the conduit and the messenger and just interpret based on what is happening to the individual at that moment and time and moving forward, without them telling me. I can see obstacles and choices you have that I will not make for you.

We all have free will and choice. For instance, if I see a police car pulling you over after happy hour and giving you a ticket or worse, chances are you have used your free will and choice. What happens as a result of your irresponsibility is on you. If someone read for me and told me I would get a DUI, I would not be getting behind the wheel of any vehicle after having drinks anywhere.

Some clients want me to make decisions for them. However, I do not do that but am an additional tool to help you figure out your journey if you are standing at a crossroad, making a major decision or just plain stuck. I am not a fixer, but I am a messenger. Do not shoot the messenger!

When I am doing my job, I have no opinion, nor am I a therapist. It is your session, not mine. It is not my job to inflict my opinion on what choices you make.
Skepticism is healthy. A little goes a long way.

THE THEORY

There is a price for power
Right now you think it is your turn
I have a theory though
Your stripes you haven't earned

There is a price for power
You can wield it either way
Mine is used for the betterment
Yours is used to slay

There is a price for power
You will never understand
Mine is a gift from God
And not to be judged by man

There is a price for power
Be careful what you do
It's transparent and sad
Your heart is not true

There is a price for power
Everyone is trying to heal
We should not judge each other
You have a heart of steel

There is a price for power
I whisper to God in heaven
And hope he hears my prayers

There is a price for power
You will never understand
People like you rarely do
I come from a place of love
I wish you could too

There is a price for power
Don't let it go to your head
I know you will read this
Remember what I have said….

Joy M. Mills
Copyright (c) 2019

Chapter Ten
Upended

The only real security is not
in owning or possessing,
not in demanding and expecting,
not in hoping, even.
Security in a relationship
lies neither in looking back to what was,
nor forward to what it might be
but living in the present and
accepting it as now.

Upended

Twenty-four years ago, I stood at the water's edge and pledged my heart, my life and my soul to you and you to me. Twenty-eight years ago, you gave me hope. Twenty-four years ago, we found courage.

I know that the most exhausting thing in life is being insecure. Our advice would be to anyone who enters into such a deep abiding commitment is if you surrender completely to the moments as they pass, you will live more richly in those moments. What we offer to each other is understanding, patience, love, openness, and the willingness to remain vulnerable.

What we found, why it has worked, and love has grown so deeply here is even if nothing else in our lives is right, you make me know without words my whole world is complete. We have always continued to seek solutions to difficult problems and work them out together.

Thank you for loving me so much and allowing me to be perfectly myself. Thank you for not trying to twist me to fit into the image the whole world believes a wife should be. Because of this, we are connected at the heart; joined at our soul. There are no boundaries or barriers for we were destined to be together.

Larry is the greatest love of my life. He has always been the man with the million-dollar smile. I could walk into a packed room and know Larry was there. He has been supportive and silently protecting me all the way through. Larry is my safe place. If you questioned him, he would tell you the same thing about me.

Larry's and my wedding was a month-long celebration, a good time and a playful time. Our vows were pledged at the water's edge, where the heavens met the earth; specifically, East Hampton, New York. Time stood still. Finally, for me, love meant something. From there, back to the middle of the country for a large reception with family and friends dancing and drinking the night away. We then jet-setted off to Scottsdale, Arizona at the Princess Hotel for our honeymoon and a well-deserved rest. These were things every little girl dreams of. Never apologize for being more than what you thought you should be.

Courage is a decision; fear is a reaction. I had the courage to marry again - this time with a completely different outcome. My fears set aside; our life began. That Fall, we bought a house, and everyone settled in for what was to be an epic future.

Here is the part where your life can change with one phone call, and it did. Larry had been having some stomach issues we had been addressing along the way with no harm, no foul results. Eighteen short, wonderful months later, boom! I received a phone call from Larry's doctor.

In those days, they could tell the spouse pretty much anything. Some biopsies had been taken from Larry, and the result was esophageal cancer. The kind of cancer that moves like wildfire and survival is dismal. If it had not been for my work and the people I met as a result of my work, we would not have had the same outcome as we have had.

Frozen sections of his biopsies were sent off to Washington state, and a phone call was made to set up a consult with the leading foremost expert in the country for Barrett's esophagus and esophageal cancers. Through that teleconference, it was decided our only option was for Larry to have transthoracic esophagectomy looping, also known as Ivor Lewis esophagectomy, a procedure where part of the esophagus is removed. The stomach is made into a cylinder, pulled up into the chest and connected to the remaining section of the esophagus. After all, this surgery was not for the faint of heart, a grave deal. We did not know if Larry was going to survive. A shout out to Larry. He exercised, was an exceptional golfer and did not smoke or drink.

The statistics were staggering, and the prognosis was poor. I did not want to add widow to my resume. Was this God's idea of a cruel joke? Through our tears, Larry's question was, "Who is going to take care of you now?" As always, he was thinking of me. I said, "No one is going to die. You are not getting off with eighteen months. You have a life sentence with me. You jump, I jump." I then prayed.

We both are realists and knew the cards were stacked against us, but I never felt it was the end for him or us as a couple. Call me delusional, but that is where I was at the time.

Larry survived the surgery after eighteen long hours in the OR. The most shocking part for me was the doctor told me they were able to save Larry's voicebox. Funny, it had never dawned on me that I might not hear my precious Larry tell me he loved me ever again.

As a result of this horrific surgery, by definition, Larry would suffer bouts of anorexia nervosa. With the team of people I compiled, we figured out a way that could possibly save my husband's life. The stomach pocket built for Larry was paralyzed and never did work. I can tell you the nurses in our house were permanent fixtures, part of the furniture and part of the family for the next fifteen years of our marriage. We had each other's back. We were able to laugh, play and travel except for the addition of one blue backpack connected to a tube that ran into a port in Larry's chest that was part of our daily routine. It contained nutrients to feed him. A small price to pay considering the alternative. We received a miracle, and it has continued to play out to this day.

Here is what I know now:

I recall a conversation. Someone said to me, "I pray all of the time. God never answers me. If our prayers aren't answered, should we keep praying?"

Fundamentally, I believe the person was wondering whether having a prayer go seemingly unanswered means that we should stop praying for that intention altogether.

My initial answer was, "No, don't stop praying. Don't ever stop praying." There is more to it than that.

When our prayers continue to go unanswered, I think it is a good time to consider then whether God may be willing something else in our life. I do not mean to say it in a way to suggest that your intention is not good, but sometimes, even when our intention is good, God knows what is better than good. He knows what is best. We have to trust that.

When I changed my prayers, my prayers eventually changed me. I have learned in the past years that praying is not so we can get what we are asking for. Praying is meant to transform us. It brings us closer to God. Praying does not exist so we can control God. It exists so that we can open our hearts to be led by Him.

Does God still perform miracles today? God miraculously heals some while choosing not to heal others for His divine purpose. No one would accuse the Apostle Paul of having weak faith, yet God refused to heal him after he asked three times.

In God's higher wisdom, He knows who and what to heal and what is best for the believer in choosing not to heal someone. Yes, I believe miracles still happen, but they are not at the direction or discretion of believers but a decision of God alone.

I believe the greatest miracle of all is that converting a blind sinner to see their sin and to change their human heart from one of serving the God of the world and seeing that they are in need of the savior, Jesus Christ. Then I believe God always answers you. We just do not always like His answer. My youngest son put it best: when the student is taking a test, the teacher is always quiet.

Chapter Eleven
A Godwink

One day your life will flash before your eyes. Make sure it is worth watching.

A Godwink

You are at a point on your journey, and the way you think things should be gets derailed. This sudden transformation is difficult to process. You feel shocked, scared and concerned or uncertain. When someone you love falls ill, gets into an accident or receives a scary health diagnosis, it is never easy. It may be the hardest thing you ever have to face. Unfortunately, it is also inevitable that we all will have to deal with this situation in life.

In the early hours of March 1, 2019, my husband yelled out my name as if his life was dependent on me helping him. It was. Between what was happening, trying to remain calm for him with 911 on the line, and the minutes ticking by as if they were hours waiting for help to arrive, life as we knew it would never be the same.

My precious Larry was bleeding out from our bedroom to our bathroom. It looked like there had been a stabbing. As a result of that big surgery, we were standing at the precipice that could steal his life. There was an erosion in the fold of the sleeve that had eaten through to the aorta. Every second counted.

The first day in the hospital, the bleeding could not be controlled. He had lost two-thirds of his blood volume. It seemed they could not put whole blood in fast enough.

Here is how God works. Larry survived the first night only because they were giving him whole blood. On what was the next day, a quiet Saturday morning in the hospital setting, and downstairs on the lower floor, it seemed almost peaceful. A team of three arrived, including a veteran doctor of twenty-nine years who understood Larry's anatomy, a calming nurse and an anesthesiologist, one of the kindest men I have ever known. The three of them as a team assured me they were going to take good care of Larry and not come out of the OR until they found and fixed the bleed. This procedure was dangerous, and Larry could ill afford to lose any more blood. They all but turned him upside down and in the very last fold they checked, they found the erosion and the bleed itself and took care of it.

We received a Godwink that day. The anesthesiologist asked if he could have a minute of my time. I stepped out to have a conversation with him. He said he remembered me even if I did not recognize him. He started with, "Thank you for saving my marriage."

I was gobsmacked. My mind was reeling. I had no idea what he meant.

He said, "My wife, along with me (as skeptical as I was), came to you many years ago separately and you pointed us in the right direction so we could begin to heal our marriage. I told myself if I ever could do anything for you, I would do everything in my power to help you. I would pay it forward. Prior to the surgery, I looked in your eyes, and I knew it was you, Joy Mills. It was my opportunity to help."

I thanked him, he thanked me, and we hugged.

It is funny how God works.

My husband being critically ill with what was a catastrophic event for the second time in our marriage has made me take a closer look at priorities. There have been other times that were heady, but nothing like this.

When you are younger, you visualize a picture of what your life would be like in five years. You fantasize about your future. You imagine peace, health and happiness. Fast forward twenty-five years, your life is nothing like you imagined. The onset of my husband's recent health scare was a not so gentle reminder of what I was not doing right, not taking care of myself and reminding me that life is fragile.

Here is what I know now:

There is a fallacy in permanence. When we start to believe something will last forever, we set ourselves up for disappointment and suffering because nothing lasts forever. Impermanence is a fundamental truth. Our relationships, the circumstances, and situations in which we find ourselves, everything around us - all of it eventually changes.

We all take things for granted, especially things that seem everlasting. Things seem permanent, so we convince ourselves they are. When something is new, it stands out, and we pay lots of attention to it. When the novelty wears off, our attention weakens, and we move on to something else.

There are two days in every week which we have no control over: yesterday and tomorrow. Today is the only day we can change.

Other people out there are praying for those things you are taking for granted. Life is often far from what we wish it to be. It is the state of dissatisfaction that keeps many of us from enjoying the ride. The starting line for contentment is embracing what is.

Whatever is right for your soul, do that.

We are not human beings having a spiritual experience. We are spiritual beings having a human experience. Death is part of that human experience, and God will be there to help us navigate our lives when it touches us.

Chapter Twelve
Save a Seat at the Table

Yes, I overthink, but not because I want to be sad. I feel too much. I value emotions, people and promises.

Life is messy. It is confusing.
It hurts.

Save a Seat at the Table

After the publication of the first book of this series, *I Wish Death Would Take A Vacation - My Story*, so many have sat before me, days or weeks after their mothers' death. I never dreamt my story would continue with an addendum, helping lead the way for what was going to be one of the darkest and most arduous journeys for many: the death of their moms.

Recently I had a conversation with a friend whose own mother lay dying and that conversation found its way into this book. It is important. She asked me through her tears, "Was it going to continue to hurt this badly? Is my mom going to be alone? I don't know what it is going to be like." My response was, "Everyone grieves differently; this is my experience only. I am praying for you."

My mother's death, as of this writing, will be rolling up on the third anniversary although my memories of the days and weeks that led up to her death have somewhat faded. My feelings of sorrow are bone-deep. I do not need to remember with any amount of clarity to feel the overwhelming sadness.

There was a point a year or so ago that I believed I would someday be beyond the bewilderment of grief. I remember all too well walking down a long hallway learning my mother was dying. At the time of my mother's death, I kissed her cheek and whispered in her ear, "Save a seat at the table."

I am a paradox of conflicting emotions, which is confusing. If I did not know it was normal to experience grief years after a loss, I think I would be feeling pretty crazy about now. It just rolls in like a slow-motion tsunami and carries you off down the shore. You might find yourself removed from the extreme intensity of grief as time goes by. The distance is a loss that needs to be grieved, but on the other side of the paradox is the reality that so many roads still lead back to her. God is amazing. How awesome is God that He allowed me to be there for my mother when she needed me most. The beautiful pain is not the end of the relationship, but it is the beginning of God's love. God was there when I took my first breath, and God was there when she took her last. She was not alone. We worship a living King.

What I know about grief is in the Bible. Deuteronomy 31:8: "The Lord himself goes before you and will be with you; he will never leave you nor forsake you. Do not be afraid; do not be discouraged."

Losing anyone you love is a sacrifice, but God made a sacrifice of His own, the life of His son Jesus Christ. All we have to do is follow Jesus directly to the Father to whom we belong for eternity.

My hope and prayer were that my words would be comforting in some minor way to carry her through what I already understood would be one of the darkest journeys of her lifetime.

Here is what I know now:

Make your mess your message.

I was thinking about the past and present, and since my mother's death, I have managed to survive almost three full laps around the sun. I realize now it is a tug of war that can go on literally for decades. The paradox is that so much and so little has changed.

Honoring past relationships has proven to have significant restorative power. You do not think about the task of mourning relationships until you have succumbed to the dark hole of grief.

I used to have this thing of being afraid to mention my mom for fear of making people uncomfortable. I mean death is awkward and depressing even when you know you will see them again.

Someone told me it was better to celebrate your loved one's birthday and I agree. One person had said she dreaded the death anniversary date so much; she realized it had been forgotten about until she looked at the calendar. They found this a positive step in healing but yet felt guilty for not remembering.

Grief is working through and adjusting to the idea our loved ones are not physically here with us any longer. That takes time. I can tell you everyone is different. We all do not live the same. We all do not grieve the same. We all do not laugh the same. We are not the same. The event of death defines a before and after and past and present.

The myth of closure is the hardest pill to swallow if you loved them. You get through it, not over it, and this is a huge accomplishment.

For all of you grieving, I am sorry for your loss. For those of you not grieving, do not squander your opportunities. For me, I wish death would take a vacation.

Chapter Thirteen
The Whole Universe is Yours

My life is the evidence of things hoped for, and it is the substance of things not known.

The Whole Universe is Yours

At the beginning of my life, it was a deck stacked against me. I had a brain that functioned and was given a gift that allowed me the ability to figure things out. It took decades.

Dramatic attempts at becoming a new person tend to end in disappointment. No matter how well you transform your appearance, behavior, talk and habits, your old self is still there.

You may be feeling a little pissy about shoving your old self in the closet. I might add so your new self can shine. Eventually, the old self crawls back into view. So, you talk a little louder, try a little harder, make happier sounds until you sound anxious and conflicted to everyone you meet. You did not do the work. Each day is a new beginning, a new chance, and a new opportunity for you to create something better and something unique.

I want to strongly recommend you bring your current rut loving self with you to work, to live side by side with your brand-new rut breaking self. If you try to leave your old self behind, it will find and haunt you. You will feel weird about your new life. You will feel angry at yourself for sometimes viewing all of the things you once loved as expendable. These things are likely to happen either way, but the experience will be harder if you do not anticipate it.

Use your times of quiet and private laziness to fuel your brave outgoing bursts of covering new ground. Reward periods of hard work with small indulgences. Once you have managed to find balance in your life, you develop the ability to savor the work and the reward. You savor the courage, and you will no longer have to savor the fear. You will be proud of your toughness and also proud of your ability to remain vulnerable and open despite all you have been through in life.

Occasionally you will get stuck a little. What you will not do is avoid the world again.

These things will not stay boxed up for long. I did that over and over in my twenties and part of my thirties. I kept turning over a new leaf. Everything was much better than a few months ago. Everything I did a few months ago was stupid, messy and ridiculous.

Fear and faith cannot live side by side. You have to pick a lane and stay in it. Never apologize for being more than you believed you should be.

Here is what I know now:

The unhappiest people in the world are the people who care too much what others think. We do not need to please anyone but ourselves. A simple rule everyone can understand is if we try to impress at any cost, we are disguising ourselves.

If we disguise ourselves, our essence dies. No one deserves to hide his or her true self, emotions or thoughts. What people say and do to you is much more about them than you. People's reactions to you are about their perspectives, wounds and experiences.

Whether people think you are amazing or believe you are the worst is more about them and how they view the world. Now, I am not saying we should be self-indulged narcissists and ignore all of the opinions and commentary we receive from others. I am merely saying incredible amounts of hurt, disappointment and sadness in our lives come directly from our tendency to take things personally. In most cases, it is far more productive and healthier to let go of other people's good or bad opinions of you and to operate with your intuition and wisdom as your guide.

IN MEMORIAM FOR FIREBALL

When you bring a pet into your life, you begin a journey. A journey that will bring you more love and devotion than you have ever known; yet, it also tests your strength and courage.

I am not naive to the sting of death. I am acutely aware of how grief impacts every part of your life. Grief stains everything.

If you pay attention and learn well when this journey is made, you will not just be a better person, but the person your pet always knew you to be. I must caution you that this journey is not without pain. Like all paths of true love, the pain is part of loving. For as surely as the sun sets, one day, your dear animal companion will follow a path you cannot yet go down. You will have to find love and strength to let them go.

A pet's time on earth is far too short. We borrow them for awhile. During those brief years, they are generous enough to give us all of their love, every inch of their spirit and heart.

When the time comes and the road curves ahead to a place we cannot see, we give one final gift and let them run ahead, young and whole once more. Godspeed sweet Fireball.

Epilogue

Everyone on the planet and I mean everyone has fears. It is not something to be ashamed of - perfect people do not exist in the world. Standing at a crossroad, think of the worst possible outcome or worst-case scenario. You would still be able to find a way out and what direction to take.

It takes courage to admit your flaws. When we uncover what is stopping us, we will find bigger and better options. Some feel stuck because they have made a series of bad decisions. You feel like you do not deserve to be happy, and you are not good enough.

We live in a culture that celebrates progress, achievement and forward movement. It is incredibly challenging to gift us the space that is needed to understand why we are feeling this way. Instead, we push the feelings down.

Learn to quiet the clamor of all the white noise around you. Replace your thoughts with the truth of who you are today. For instance, I am enough. I have options. I have an abundance. I am not alone. Engage in the wanderlust. Enjoy the little things. These are rare opportunities we give ourselves.

We are human, and we need to break the routine. God has your back if you learn to listen. It may not be the life you expected, but it is the life you were given. Your life is in progress. Your imperfect life is messy. Show up anyway.

I have learned when you show up fully, take a deep breath, and receive open-armed the humble gifts of an ordinary day. Your mind will slow, your heart will expand, and you will remember today is enough.

I had not updated my narrative to who I am today. I am the hero of my story. I gave myself grace through my imperfections.

Afterword

For me, death pulled the trigger on my past and where it took me. What I have learned with vacations, you only unpack for a minute. Then the trip is over, and life continues.

Stop being the victim. When you get into the mindset of the victim, you often find your thoughts lead back to past traumas. Your mind becomes plagued by these thoughts, and you find yourself thinking everything always goes wrong for you. Of course, this is not the case at all because you are in control of your life.

You should not think that because you have failed before, you will fail now. True forgiveness is when you say thank you for the experience. The past is a place of reference, not a place of residence.

Bibliography

- *I Wish Death Would Take A Vacation – My Story (A Mini Menoir – Part One)*
  ISBN: 978-0-9854367-1-1

- *Between Heaven and Earth: The Soul Purpose* (Alone at the Crossroads)
  ISBN: 0-9671280-0-5

- *The Mystical Side of Reality* (Audiocassette)
  ISBN: 0-9671280-1-3

- *Why Are We Here? (An Honest Truth)* (E-Book and CD)
  ISBN: 0-9671280-2-1

- *Destination Spirituality: A Guide Toward Inner Peace* (Paperback)
  ISBN: 0-9671280-8-0

- *Desperation, Fear and Love: The Great Motivators*
  ISBN: 0-9671280-6-4

- *Raw Emotion: When Time Stands Still* (E-Book and 2 CD Set)
  ISBN: 0-9671280-7-2

Other Works by Joy M. Mills
(Including Bibliographic References)

TELEVISION/RADIO APPEARANCES

- ABC KDNL 30 St. Louis The Allman Report
- CNN – America's Talking
- FX Breakfast Time
- CBS – The Gordon Elliott Show
- Aura Television (New York Cable)
- NBC – The Other Side
- ABC – Turning Point
- CNN – Talk Radio
- TLC – "Crossing Over" with John Edward
- Sirius Radio – The Laura Smith Show

LECTURES/WORKSHOPS

- Band Wagon Promotions (People of Like Mind Expositions) (Illinois and Missouri)
- Psychics, Seers, and Mystics (New York and Canada)
- Whole Life and Whole Health Expositions (New York, California, Massachusetts, Illinois, Florida, and Georgia)
- Joy Mills Workshops (Missouri, New York, California, Florida, Ohio)
- Universal of Light Expos (Ohio)

MEDIA PUBLICATIONS

- Articles about Joy Mills in Missouri/Illinois Newspapers
- Country magazine, the Hamptons, New York

- St. Louis magazine, August 1999
- St. Louis magazine, columnist, March 2001 through December 2003

BOOKS

- *I Wish Death Would Take A Vacation – My Story (A Mini Menoir – Part One)*
  ISBN: 978-0-9854367-1-1

- *Between Heaven and Earth: The Soul Purpose (Am I Good Enough?)*
  ISBN: 978-0-9671280-9-2

- *Between Heaven and Earth: The Soul Purpose (Alone at the Crossroads)*
  ISBN: 0-9671280-0-5

- *The Mystical Side of Reality* (Audiocassette)
  ISBN: 0-9671280-1-3

- *Why Are We Here? (An Honest Truth)* (Audiocassette)
  ISBN: 0-9671280-3-X

- *Why Are We Here? (An Honest Truth)* (E-Book and CD)
  ISBN: 0-9671280-2-1

- *Life, Death and Miracles* (E-Book and CD)
  ISBN: 0-9671280-4-8

- *Destination Spirituality: A Guide Toward Inner Peace* (Hardback)
  ISBN: 1-4010-7661-0

- *Destination Spirituality: A Guide Toward Inner Peace* (Paperback)
  ISBN: 0-9671280-8-0

- *Desperation, Fear and Love: The Great Motivators*
  ISBN: 0-9671280-6-4

- *Raw Emotion: When Time Stands Still* (E-Book and 2 CD Set)
  ISBN: 0-9671280-7-2

Resources

Arch Phys Med Rehabil. Author manuscript; available in PMC 2015 Jul 27.
Published in final edited form as:
Arch Phys Med Rehabil. 2014 Jun; 95(6): 1223–1224.
doi: 10.1016/j.apmr.2013.06.002

Moody Bible Institute
820 N. LaSalle Street
Chicago, Illinois 60610

Long considered the gold standard of Bible-based education, Moody Bible Institute has been preparing students for ministry since 1886, with a combination of biblical knowledge and practical training.

St. Louis History Museum Archives
5700 Lindell Boulevard
St. Louis, Missouri 63112

Missouri Department of Social Services Children's Division
Main Office
205 Jefferson Street
Jefferson City, Missouri 65101

Chicago History Museum - Transportation
1601 N. Clark Street
Chicago, Illinois 60610

National Suicide Prevention Lifeline
1-800-273-8255 (1-800-273-TALK)

National Hopeline Network
1-800-784-2433 (1-800-SUICIDE)

Child Abuse Hotline
1-800-422-4453

National Domestic Violence Hotline
1-800-799-7233
www.thehotline.org

Partnership for Drug-Free Kids
1-855-DRUGFREE or text your message to 55753

Rape, Abuse, Incest, National Network (RAINN)
1-800-656-HOPE (1-800-656-4673)

Sexual Abuse – Stop It Now!
1-888-PREVENT

National Alliance on Mental Illness (NAMI)
1-800-950-6264
www.nami.org

Anxiety/Panic Disorder Information Hotline
1-800-64-PANIC

Depression and Bipolar Support Alliance (DBSA)
www.dbsalliance.org

What People Are Saying

"Joy is an amazing mentor, a woman of great courage, and a true friend. Through Joy, I have learned that sometimes things are not always as they seem, and that the answers to our questions will come in their own time if we pay attention to what is happening around us.

A woman with enormous courage to share her history, Joy has lived through many challenging situations in her lifetime, yet survived where others may have crumbled. Combined with her gift and the wisdom gained from each negative situation, she knows, and understands what others are going through and offers insights with compassion and empathy. In her readings, Joy tells what needs to be told without the sugar coating, but with refreshing and sometimes surprising observations. Joy calls it as she sees it, and serves it up with levity and humor where appropriate.

In this complicated and sometimes unforgiving world, I am grateful that Joy is here and offers wise counsel and hope where sometimes it seems things are hopeless."

~Pam P.

"This is a true account of a young life on the edge. Every obstacle thrown at her with the page turning act of overcoming. This is a story of resiliency and support from unexpected places. Woven with humor and humility, this book was written not to bemoan a fate but to share hope that any circumstance can be overcome and overcome with great success. It is both fascinating and uplifting."

~Lisa K.

"Joy and I have been with each other through the highs and lows of life from raising kids and grandkids to losing loved ones. I met her in a professional setting but I now know her personally and what is amazing about Joy is that no matter what happens in life, Joy's friendships, her faith, and most of all, her love for others is what gets her through it all. She is one of the most giving, kind souls I have ever met and her positive energy, her words and her gifts that she gives each day is precisely what the world needs.

Joy's book, I Wish Death Would Take A Vacation – My Story is a must read to anyone who is questioning death, the why, and the what now. Having lost my husband and both of my parents, I related closely to the raw, real, gut wrenching, dark, emotional roller coaster that comes after losing a loved one. Joy was able to put into words emotions that I felt after those losses but could never quite describe or understand. It helped me find comfort as well as meaning to my own experiences.

Grief never really goes away. You get through each death. You never really get over it."

~Debbie O.

"Joy Mills is a consummate professional in her field. Upon meeting her, she is reserved, courteous, and will weigh her words carefully with you. After you've been read a couple of times, and she learns your personality, she will give you a pack for your punch! She is a tender but tough soul, who has been through a lot in her life, thereby understanding how much her clients need from her at their readings. I'm glad I was referred to her as a client over ten years ago, as she was an immense source of help to me with learning to walk through my husband's suicide. I'm proud to now be able to call her my friend.

I Wish Death Would Take A Vacation – My Story is a book written for those who have struggled with feelings of worthiness, worthlessness, restlessness, sadness, or just plain "stuck" in your lives. If you're at an emotional crossroad in your life, pick up this book. I read this book in a day and a half (which for me is a feat, in and of itself!) All of us have the "stories of our lives", but after reading this book, it left me with more feelings and emotions than I knew how to articulate. So, I just stayed alone with them for a day. This true story of struggle and survival hits on all key facets of life. It is raw, it is real, and the author tells it with a tongue-in-cheek flair. It is a book of trepidation and inspiration! Looking forward to her next book!"

~Maria B.

"The day I met Joy Mills, it changed my life forever. I still recall when our paths crossed in 2006, as if it were yesterday. I was astonished by her gift of clairvoyance, her passion to help people, and her dedication to guide me down life's journey. Our paths have continued to cross over the years, and she truly has been given a fabulous gift from the Universe. I have been blessed to work with Joy on a regular basis. She never tells you what you want to hear, but will always tell you what you need to hear. I have received phenomenal advice from her that has helped me in both my life and career. Whether seeing her for a psychic session, reading one of her books, or having a drink with her over some laughs, she is always at her best. There is no doubt that Joy has left a fingerprint on my life that will never be erased…. Anyone that crosses Joy's path has been given a great gift from the Universe! I am truly blessed to call her my friend."

~Laurie C

"Joy Mills has the gift of pure insight! Unparalleled to any other I have seen or witnessed. Joy shares her gift, much like herself, with wisdom, Love, knowledge and great authenticity. My personal readings with Joy, like the truth, have been scary real, cathartic, loving, insightful, tough and uplifting. I am grateful for Joy and her gift."

~Cate M.

"There are a few people one meets along their journey that can be trusted to help guide them through the wormholes of life's biggest moments. Joy is one of those people. Firmly connected to a universal kindness and love, Joy has always met her own craggy life moments head-on and helped me do the same. Having walked through an intense and rapid-fire period of grief recently (Mother, Sister, Father and Beloved Dog). I have learned just how valuable it is to have a friend and mentor like Joy.

Pain of loss, especially of a parent/Mother, who walked through life damaged herself, brought up a kaleidoscope of feelings for me. Some days truly were diamonds and some days were surly stones. Walking through these times was made easier with the help of Joy's wisdom, calm understanding and practical advice. It has always been Joy's purpose to be of service to all she meets. She shines on for many of us, helping to lead our way out of pain and into love and growth.

Joy's last book; I Wish Death Would Take A Vacation, she took us on the wild ride of a girlhood fraught with abandonment and cruelty. It is clear that her intention in writing the book was purely to help others see that life can throw all its darkness at a person, so that there are really only two choices: stay with the darkness because it feels normal or break free and find a light so pure that only love gets through.

Joy meets her past (in the book) and her life with equal amounts of humor and barefaced truth. In my own journey I have met several people with a strong connection to ancestors and the light of Source/God. I can honestly say that Joy is one of a kind. Where others might have personal agendas or be working with fear, Joy works only with love. Her consulting/conversation is direct, honest, helpful, forthright and so incredibly accurate it never ceases to amaze. Being around Joy, one feels a strong sense of love and calm.

Joy values people. She values her life lessons because they give her great empathy for those that come to her in their own troubles. This empathy gives her an amazing ability to help guide others.

She values time: her own and her client's. She values people who seek out truth and that spread care and kindness. She values accuracy. She values kindness and demonstrates it every day.

Her life has been a difficult one but a mighty one, an inspirational life. I am better for having known her and been gifted with all her accurate and useful guidance over the years. Her books are a testament to a life well lived…despite it all."
~Ann F

"I've known Joy 35+ years, shortly before this book was written I myself had been going through a grieving period with the loss of my mother. Joy helped me navigate a very difficult time in my life and put things into perspective. We all carry around baggage and trauma from childhood and or family. Joy is a great example of how one can endure the worst and still change the course of life to be great no matter what hand you are dealt. Joy brings home the real deal in dealing with family and the trauma of a child having to constantly shuffle from place to place. This hit close to home for me as we experienced foster care children in our home for respite care and fully understood Joy's story and the children that live this nightmare. Thanks to the book I too hate Ms. Rita. This book is not to be missed, I couldn't put the book down and have been eagerly awaiting the next book."

~Gina C.

"Joy Mills told me about a path for my life and I didn't believe her. That was 25 years ago and sure enough, despite my best efforts, she nailed it. The best thing that came out of our talks? Our friendship. Her compassion, support, and insights are invaluable. Joy is so well respected in her field and yet few people know that her life has been a series of struggles that would break most people. And yet, her life is devoted to helping the rest of us see more clearly, and to be more kind and forgiving with each other."

~Helen M. T

"I Wish Death Would Take A Vacation by Joy M. Mills takes a step away from spiritual healing and is a glimpse into the continuing journey of Joy's life. This book puts an emotional and human connection to the name behind the many books she's written. She took a step away from her helping and healing ways to rip open old wounds and expose her real and true self to her readers. An exceptionally well written memoir shows the raw and real Joy Mills, and shows us that despite her gift, she is human just like all of us."

~KK

"This book was gifted to me recently and I cannot recommend it enough. It is beautifully written and eloquently captures vulnerable moments in the author's life. Throughout the book you will find stories about her life, her reflections on these experiences and the broader lessons that can be derived from them. Beautiful and insightful poetry is also interwoven throughout the chapters. This book is something that many people will be able to relate to as well as find comfort in and meaning for their own experiences. I could not put this book down once I picked it up, and I am left wanting to know more about the life of Joy Mills and how her experiences have led her to fulfill her potential, despite all odds. I found myself rereading many passages as I reflected on my own life experiences, especially with family. If you buy any book this year - buy this one."

~Blair P.

A Note from The Author

I had not updated my narrative to who I am today. I am the hero of my story. I am enough.

My narrative has evolved and changed. The way I live my life now compared to my early years, I am aware of what I am doing, and I own my stuff so others can make better decisions and see they, too, can climb out of anything. You do not have to carry it alone. You can open your arms wide, the good and the bad of it, and become better people.

About the Author

Joy M. Mills is an internationally known clairvoyant who has written, lectured and taught over many years. She has done numerous television appearances, radio and magazine articles. Joy is a published author, whose books and CDs are sold throughout the world in bookstores and online.

Joy resides with her husband and family in the St. Louis area where she teaches and maintains a private practice.